TRUTH ABOUT TONGUES

HUGH F. PYLE

ACCENT BOOKS
Denver, Colorado

MEMBER OF
EVANGELICAL CHRISTIAN
PUBLISHERS ASSOCIATION

Accent Publications
12100 W. Sixth Avenue
P.O. Box 15337
Denver, Colorado 80215

Copyright © 1976 B/P Publications, Inc.

Printed in U.S.A.

Library of Congress Catalog Card Number: 76-8730

ISBN 916406-19-9

Foreword

This is a rough day for many Christians! It is a day crowded with all kinds of strange teachings—teachings that lead away from the plain fundamentals of the infallible Word of God. Satan is busy in this century seeking to confuse good, sincere believers. His success is obvious—all about us are weakened churches and defeated, unsettled, baby Christians.

I commend this book by Dr. Hugh Pyle for I believe it will answer the questions being raised today relative to the tongues movement. With plain, frank, lucid words he deals with the subject. Illustrations are prolific.

The last paragraph of the book gives the spirit of the author. Dr. Pyle says, "Though I have spoken honestly and plainly, it is with a sincere desire to help lead people into a knowledge of the truth. Many sweet Christians are nevertheless ill-taught and deceived. The time is short to serve the Lord and reach this sin-sick world with the glorious gospel."

Prepare yourself now to read a book that will open your eyes and your heart; yes, read and receive a clear understanding of the subject: *Truth About Tongues*.

Lee Roberson, Pastor
Highland Park Baptist
Church
Chattanooga, Tennessee

Preface

What is the real truth? Who has the answer?

Why the present tangle over tongues? Consider these questions:

How can Pentecostals, Roman Catholics, Episcopalians, Jesus freaks, hippies, long-haired effeminate males, night-club entertainers, religious liberals and rock musicians all have the same "religious" experience?

If this is a bona fide experience, why did Jesus not speak in tongues, nor advocate it?

Why is it never mentioned in any letter to the New Testament churches except Corinth—the carnal, "baby" church?

What kind of "tongues" experience do the Hindus, the Buddhists and other non-Christians have? How do Spiritists and Mormons pull it off?

Why did Mark alone mention the word "tongues" among all of the Gospel writers, and that only once?

Why did the great Spirit-filled soul winners of history carefully avoid telling us about tongues if they are important?

Why do the leading men among fundamental, soul-winning churches and the great evangelists of today never speak in tongues?

Why do the charismatics not use their "tongues" gift to carry the gospel to those of other languages on foreign mission fields?

What brings about the use of such unscriptural terms as "getting the baptism," "seeking the gifts," or "initial evidence"?

If this tongues experience is really a "Pentecostal" experience, then where are the visible "tongues of fire" sitting on them, and where is the rushing mighty wind filling the house? More important, why do not we witness the genuine salvation of multitudes of souls, as at Pentecost?

Why are so many women involved in tongues when the plain command of Paul in I Corinthians 14 was ". . . let the women keep silence"?

Why do all subsequent references to God's gifts in the Bible never include tongues? And why is it not mentioned as a "fruit of the spirit" in Galatians 5?

These are just some of the questions we'll find answered as we search them out together.

Let's be honest enough to look at experiences in the light of the Bible instead of looking at the Bible in the light of one's experience.

Hugh F. Pyle
Panama City, Florida

Contents

Chapter 1

HOW CAN THESE THINGS BE?

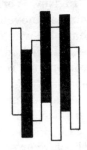

A young wife in Florida goes into ecstasy over her "tongues" experience, leaves her fundamental church, breaks up her home and divorces her husband because he will not renounce his Bible convictions and join her in the "charismatic" (tongues) movement.

A missionary couple who had been greatly used of God was drawn into the "tongues" experience. Home on furlough, they have kept putting off going back to the mission field for years now, while engaging in charismatic meetings. Thus the heathen in the jungles have lost their missionaries who had been such a blessing before.

A Pennsylvania pastor withdraws from the tongues people after serving for twenty years as a Pentecostal pastor. Seeing the inconsistencies of the movement and realizing that the so-called "interpretations" didn't measure up, he began to study his Bible and came out of the tongues group.

In New York, a lady who was once in the tongues movement told me that she feels now that she was certainly "obsessed" if not possessed with demons, and now she expresses tremendous relief to be delivered from the experience.

A saved Pentecostal, seeking the tongues experience, found the genuine Spirit-filled life instead. He had gone through a Pentecostal Bible school, ever seeking. When he broke with the charismatics, he joined a Bible church and is now a successful missionary in Brazil. He declares that the *true* Spirit-filled life led him AWAY from the Pentecostal movement!

Roman Catholic charismatic leader Kevin Ranaghan of Notre Dame says:

> There should be a charismatic renewal of other Christian churches into one world-wide church. We must work concretely for the union of all those churches involved in the charismatic renewal—not just the Catholic church, but all Christian churches (*FEA News and Views,* October, 1974).

An emotional lady who once attended a fundamental, soul-winning Baptist church was led off by others into what she believed would be a more fervent and spiritual church. After two years of terrifying experiences, during which time she alienated her unsaved sons and lost her reason, she has finally received medical help, but comes to church staring straight ahead like a "zombie."

Missionaries from the Orient were persuaded, along with their Lancaster, Pennsylvania, pastor, to attend a tongues service. One woman poured forth a torrent of words which the interpreter said was Chinese. Later the missionaries told the pastor that it was indeed Chinese—the most indescribable filth and profanity that could be phrased in the Chinese language!

A Canadian pastor, who for eight years was a Pentecostal, now says that the tongues experience was just "the flesh" in his case, according to Evangelist Fred Brown; while still another pastor in Colorado, also a convert from the Pentecostal movement, says he is convinced *his* "tongues" episode was the work of the devil.

A student told Dr. Kurt Koch that he had been invited by his friends to a conference of the Pentecostal church in Ireland. He was urged to pray for "the gift." Some days later one of the speakers laid his hands on him. He experienced a warm sensation going through him and he began to "speak in tongues." He had no idea what he was saying, but his emotions were stirred. After a few weeks he no longer had any desire to read his Bible or pray and he lost his original assurance of salvation. He confessed to Dr. Koch that through the "gift" of tongues he had lost his peace with God. It was only after he denounced this experience that he received his peace and assurance again.

A young man just left my presence. He related that as a teenager he had been invited to a Pentecostal meeting. People were being urged to go to the front and pray at the altar for one thing or another. As a young Christian, he felt he should go forward and pray for his father. But as he knelt, several men gathered around him and began to pray in a babble of confused sounds.

Then the evangelist came down and stood right in front of him and cried, "Young man, speak in tongues!" He was frightened and had no idea what to do or what he had encountered. Then the evangelist told him to repeat some words after him. They were a gibberish of hashed phrases which the boy tried to repeat, not knowing what else to do. As he proceeded to attempt to pronounce the garbled words, the evangelist announced publicly in a loud voice, "Ladies and gentlemen, this young lad is speaking in tongues!" Needless to say, the young fellow was cured of attending Pentecostal meetings.

A minister of the High Church (Anglican) spoke in tongues and another interpreted at a large ministers' conference, according to Dr. Kurt Koch. The interpretation sounded like a few Bible verses strung together with the message that there was a difficult time ahead for the church. One minister who had witnessed the affair wondered why it was necessary to have "speaking in tongues" to hear a few verses from the Bible which they could just as well read for themselves.

In San Diego, California, a woman stayed for an after-meeting with a tongues group. Hands were placed on her that she might receive the "baptism." She fell down unconscious. When she revived, she was lying on the floor with her mouth still opening and shutting itself automatically without a word being uttered. She was terribly frightened, but was assured that she had spoken wonderfully in tongues and that now she had the Holy Spirit. Later, when she came to a man of God for counseling, she was still suffering from the bad effects of this "spiritual baptism."

A student at an English Bible college who was submerged in the "tongues" flood, declared that he did not need to read the Bible anymore. God the Father would Himself appear and speak to him. A young woman at a Scottish Bible college went several times to have the hands of a Pentecostal preacher laid on her so she could receive "the baptism of the Spirit." Finally she experienced a warm feeling which she regarded as the second blessing. Today she has slipped so far that she completely disregards praying and reading God's Word. She no longer finds it a joy to be a Christian.

Yet, in spite of all this, many people today are being assured that if they will just get this "baptism" and speak in "tongues," they will have something very wonderful and will indeed be superior Christians. What is it all about? How can these things be?

Chapter 2

CHARISMA OR CLAPTRAP?

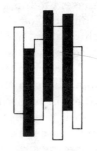

I had to find out the truth. I've always wanted all that God had in store for me. From my first complete dedication to Christ as a young man of nineteen, I determined to go all the way with the Lord. I began to devour the Scofield Reference Bible and copies of *The Sword of the Lord*. I listened eagerly to Dr. M. R. DeHaan and Evangelist Charles E. Fuller. I read every book I could find by H. A. Ironside, John R. Rice, William Pettingill. I studied D. L. Moody and Charles H. Spurgeon. I poured over the revival works of Charles Finney and George Whitefield. I read Charles Wesley, David Brainerd and Billy Sunday. I cried over souls with George Truett and Gipsy Smith. I devoured the missionary works of Jonathan Goforth, Adoniram Judson and Hudson Taylor. I read every word of McCall Barbour to be sure

I was getting all there was of the deeper life and the death-to-self philosophy. I eagerly studied the Moody Colportage books. In all of these, I found an incentive to be filled with the Spirit of God for soul-winning power. In none of these did I find any encouragement to "Pentecostalism" or the "tongues" movement.

I can truthfully say that during these thirty-four years in the ministry, Christ has been all in all to me. Having Him, I also had the wonderful presence of the indwelling Holy Spirit. He has been sufficient in every crisis. I have sometimes been a leaky vessel and have had to be filled with the Spirit over and over again, but He has always furnished the strength for the burdens and tears of the pastorate. He has supplied the power for soul winning in the many evangelistic campaigns. God has given fruit—and much joy.

From time to time I would encounter Pentecostals who felt I needed that indescribable something which they called "the second blessing," "gettin' the Holy Ghost," or "the baptism of the Spirit." I found none of these phrases or experiences in the Bible. While some thought I should have "tongues," I was well aware that I had all I could do to take care of and rightly use the one tongue God had given me!

But then the movement took on "charisma," and Pentecostalism came along with a brand new dress. It seems that liberal Lutherans, portly Presbyterians, and even eucharistic Episcopalians were speaking in tongues, and the whole ecumenical package was called the charismatic movement. Now, what was this all about? The Lutherans, at least most of them, believed in baptismal regeneration, the Presbyterians had always had a reputation for being staid and dignified, and most of the Episcopalians I had talked to through the years knew nothing of a salvation or "new birth" experience, and now suddenly they were among the spiritual aristocrats of the world—they were speaking in tongues!

Occasionally I even heard of a backslidden Baptist or some worldly, emotional (so-called) Baptist congregation that was now a part of the "charismatic movement." At long last, some began to say, revival has come to the world. Charismatic renewal was supposed to usher in a new day for the church.

But my Bible hadn't changed. I still found only a very few places in the Bible that referred to "tongues." Three of these were in Acts and one in Mark. First Corinthians dealt with the subject in two chapters, but here Paul was correcting heresy, as far as I could see, in the most carnal of all the churches mentioned in the Bible. The rest of the Bible was silent about it. Never once could I find that I was commanded to seek the "gift of tongues."

When I was converted I was immersed by the Spirit into the body of Christ, as First Corinthians 12:13 declares. I also followed the Lord in believer's baptism in water as an act of obedience, which pictured the death, burial and resurrection of Christ and my identification with Him in His death and resurrection (Colossians 2:12). Again, I know that I have been filled with the Spirit and have had special times of anointing for service and soul winning, according to the promises of such verses as Ephesians 5:18 and Acts 1:8. But in all of the Spirit's instruction to believers in this age, I found no reason to believe that I had missed some other startling and ecstatic secret of spiritual power.

Neither had the spiritual giants around me changed. The great soul winning pastors were still busy fulfilling the command of Christ—winning the lost. In fact, within the past ten years, with the charismatic crowd running full steam ahead, the sane, scriptural New Testament churches have been increasing more and more, some of them growing to previously unheard-of-greatness. In almost every state in America, the largest and fastest-growing churches have been Bible-preaching Baptist churches with the same great Bible doctrines they have always believed, not even to mention the hundreds of other solid, soul-winning churches of other denominations that are smaller but growing. How on earth have these churches made it without charismatic renewal?

Then the Roman Catholics suddenly began to speak in tongues. *The Catholic Voice* for September 19, 1974, reported: "Archbishop James Hayes of Halifax, N.D., called the charismatic movement a genuine renewal in the sense of Vatican II. . . it renews faith, love and dedication of Catholics in and for the church." The address was given before the Northeastern Regional Catholic Charismatic Conference held at Loyola College. In June, 1974, over 20,000

Pentecostal Catholics gathered at Notre Dame in Indiana. The cardinal who addressed them gave enthusiastic approval of the charismatic movement, describing the important break-throughs to bring about "Christian Unity." J. B. Williams in *Faith for the Family* (November-December, 1974) states that the same Catholic speaker addressing the Pres-byterian Charismatic Conference in March, 1974, said, "I see the heads of the Christian churches together. Let us come back home. Home means the upper room, Pentecost again." Of course, anyone who has studied church or Roman Catholic history knows that "home again" really means, "Let's get back to Rome!"

Dr. Williams continues by quoting an As-semblies of God preacher: "I know an Episcopa-lian priest in this city who is so liberal he neither believes in the virgin birth nor the res-urrection. Yet he has recently received the baptism in the Spirit and exhibits a marvelous power in his ministry!" The question arises, since an unbeliever, a Bible-denying modern-ist, is not a Christian in the Bible sense of the word, what kind of "marvelous power" does he have in his ministry? Surely not *God's* power!

A Wycliffe translator, hearing of the "speak-ing in tongues" craze, said, "Send them to us in Mexico," describing the many tribes who needed to hear the gospel. Yes, if the true gift of tongues (languages) were operating today as it did on Pentecost, the missionaries would find their work much easier. But whoever heard of a charismatic rushing out to the heathen to exercise his gift? You'll hear of this when the "faith healers" take their healing ministry to the hospital wards!

Charisma, or Claptrap? Well, I had to find out which.

Chapter 3

BIRDS BETWEEN THE RUNWAYS

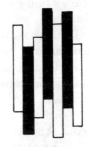

While the big jet was taxiing out the Atlanta airport runways toward take-off, I saw them. The birds were on the ground between us and the main runway where the jets ahead of us were roaring into the sky. Those birds seemed to be envying the huge planes. I'm sure it was my imagination, but they would watch a DC-10 roar into the heavens and then look back at us as if to say, "Well, when we can do *that,* we'll qualify as flyers!"

As capable as birds are, they could not take off with such power nor fly the distances and carry the loads of the super planes of the seventies.

I thought of what my little life would be without the Holy Spirit. Of how utterly futile it would be for me to even go to that revival appointment without His fullness. It would be like the little bird trying to imitate the jet.

But the jet was not just making noise and blowing smoke to show off for the birds. The planes had a cargo and passengers—and a destination.

The Spirit-filled life is wonderful indeed, and it is not just noise and smoke. Someday I hope to write a book on the Holy Spirit, and before closing this one, will give you God's divine alternative to the charismatic effort, but for the present we must stick to the subject, "The Truth About Tongues."

We have to admire the sincerity of many in the Pentecostal movement, particularly in the earlier years of the century, who have been dissatisfied to be "birds between the runways" and have longed for something better. Many of them have been dedicated Christians who love the Lord. I may disagree with their doctrine, but I commend their zeal. I'm sure a great many of them are today a bit startled that their "baptism" experience has been picked up by modernists, Catholics, Jesus freaks and night clubbers.

Books have been written by both the tongues adherents and those who disagree, telling about the 1906 Azuza Street prayer meetings in Los Angeles and the beginning of the Pentecostal movement in America. For years they were the extreme folk in the little wooden building down across the tracks. Sometimes they were called "Holy Rollers." I once peeked into a service and saw them rolling, saw people prostrate on the floor, and heard their shrieks as they groaned and cried for the spiritual experience they sought. About the nearest thing to that I could recall in my Bible was the episode on Mount Carmel when the prophets of Baal screamed and cut themselves as they shouted, "O Baal, hear us!" (I Kings 18).

Then in the early sixties the tongues movement took on respectability (with some) by suddenly capturing the fancy of Presbyterians in Hollywood and Lutherans in the Midwest.

Noted Bible teacher J. Vernon McGee writes, "The movement has spread like an epidemic of bubonic plague and it has infected those who have not been inoculated with the Word of God." Dr. McGee tells of churches split wide open in California and Honolulu because of the charismatic movement. Many of them have been torn apart. Fortunate the pastor who has so taught his people the Bible that they cannot be tossed to and fro with every wind of doctrine that comes along.

Columnist Bob McClure writes in *The Bible Trumpet,* "The modern-day tongues movement is spreading throughout Christendom with amazing speed. It is creating more excitement than any other religious movement of the twentieth century. Thousands of people in almost every denomination say they have 'spoken in tongues.' "

Editor E. L. Bynum in the *Plains Baptist Challenger* recently wrote warning us of the deceptive methods of the charismatic movement. "Especially do they gloat when they have captured a Baptist Church," he states, and then proceeds to describe such a capture of the Grant Park Baptist Church in Tampa,

Florida. The present pastor took the church without telling them that he had "received the baptism," nor did he tell them that he was praying for their young people to "get it" until the church had been engulfed in this thing. Thus we see the Fifth Column approach they frequently use.

"The charismatics want your church," Dr. Bynum writes, as he reminds us that "Deeper Life," "Full Gospel Business Men's Fellowship" and other like groups are counseling their charismatic converts to return to their denominational churches and spread the tongues speaking in its membership. Catholics, Baptists, Methodists, and Lutherans are urged to stay in their church and make it a "charismatic church."

Winning souls is one thing; gaining proselytes to a system or to an emotional experience is something else. I recall that Jesus said to some religious zealots in His day, "Woe unto you. . . for ye compass sea and land to make one proselyte, and when he is made, ye make him twofold more the child of hell than yourselves" (Matthew 23:15).

A reporter for a secular magazine made an investigation and described what he saw in a "charismatic" meeting: "They prayed in tongues, that piercing unintelligible wailing that increases in intensity minute after minute. . . I watched them, with their eyes half-closed, seemingly in a trance, their tongues moving furiously in their mouths, arms extended into the air."

I am reminded that when the Lord Jesus

wanted to perform one of His miracles He *put out* those who were wailing and making a noise (Luke 8:54).

A man of God who was once in the movement believes that since they do not understand the Bible truth of the eternal security of the believer, these Pentecostals grab onto "tongues" as a form of security, feeling that if they have this prestige "gift" they can *feel* that they are saved. So for these birds between the runways the charismatic experience has become a sort of "security blanket."

Thank God there is something better! Jesus said to one who had to have a sign or physical proof to believe, "Blessed are they that have not seen, and yet have believed" (John 20:29).

Yes, "the just shall live by *faith*."

Chapter 4

A TERRIFYING EPISODE

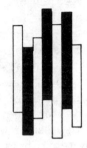

I determined in my investigation not only to read what the charismatics have said, and what Bible scholars have taught, but also to talk to those in the movement and those who have been delivered from it. One of the latter was a Christian lady in a New York city. Her troubles had crowded her to Christ.

Not long after she had received Christ, her young Lutheran minister, along with other friends, invited her to attend a "Full Gospel meeting" in Buffalo. She was destitute, unhappy and troubled, and had been saved only three weeks. During the meeting a woman stood up, babbling in strange phrases. She was informed that this was "tongues speaking." People in the congregation were urged to come up to the altar and seek "the baptism." Since the appeal was "to all who need prayer," and since her marriage was in trouble, she went up, determined to do anything to get the spiritual help she felt she needed.

As they prayed and cried over her, she lost control of her faculties, began to utter gibberish, at first aware but not in control of what she was doing. Then she passed out, and was later told that she had spoken in tongues. Over this she felt elated, since she was assured that this was a great thing in her life.

But for the next week she was sick, had fits of depression, felt like she was dying, and thought about suicide. Later she attended other prayer meetings at this pastor's home and again went into the ecstasy of "tongues." She felt "high" and was complimented for her attainment. She was puzzled, though, that the Lutheran minister told her not to "let loose" like that in his church since it might divide the church.

Her home was still broken. Her new experience had brought no help. She wondered why. Then she was invited to the home of friends who were having "charismatic" meetings. There she fell and almost went down the steps, feeling as though someone had pushed her, though there was no one close enough to have done so. Her "friends" again wanted to lay hands on her and pray for her. She felt a terrible depression and cried, "Oh, please let me out of here!"

At the home of these friends she had seen a picture, supposedly of the head of Christ. It seemed to glow and the hair grew long and the eyes seemed to pierce right through her. She felt some strange force and ended up going to a fortune teller. She felt that Satan was trying to kill her. Her husband got drunk, went after her with a knife, and then, while under the influence, drove her down highways at ninety miles per hour. She escaped from all of this, but still felt she was going to die. When she blamed the tongues experience, her charismatic friends told her she was blaspheming the Holy Spirit! She became more terrified and was paralyzed in bed for a month.

Calling a Christian friend, for the first time since her conversion she was given some good advice. She was reminded, "Greater is he that is in you, than he that is in the world" (I John 4:4), and was advised to plead the blood of Christ when Satan came to torment her. Her friend sent a godly Baptist pastor to see her (I have been with this soul-winning pastor in revival services), and she discussed her supposed "baptism" and the tongues matter with him. He gave her the Bible truth about it all. For the first time she understood.

As I interviewed this delivered lady, she made the following observations:

1. The Pentecostals had taken Scriptures out of context to build their case.

2. They had glorified her instead of Christ because she "spoke in tongues."

3. Christ was only incidental; the Holy Ghost had their main attention.

4. She did not know what she had said while

in this "tongues" state, nor did anyone else know—and no one could interpret what she said.

5. For awhile she felt she had been demon-possessed. After learning her Bible, she now concludes she was just obsessed by the devil.

6. "It was terrible, and I shudder to think back upon the experience (of tongues), but I'm glad to tell it if I can help others," she said to me as we concluded the interview.

The lady is now a happy, victorious and active member of the good, sound, church pastored by the minister who taught her the truth. An entirely different story awaits us in Chapter 5.

Chapter 5

SPIRIT FILLED!—
BUT NO "TONGUES!"

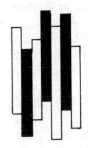

Someone asked Vance Havner if he thought the "Holy Rollers" would get to Heaven? He replied that he thought some of them would if they didn't run past it! This is the true account of a man who was seeking the experience of tongues—and ran past it!

Peter Brooks of Altoona, Pennsylvania, was saved at age ten or eleven in a Swedish Covenant church. His mother was in the holiness movement and he grew up in Nazarene and holiness doctrine. An Assemblies of God church was started in his area and the family became "Pentecostal." As a teenager, Peter Brooks began to seek the experience of "tongues," having been taught that this would be the evidence of his having the "baptism of the spirit."

He wanted to be sure of his salvation and thought that if he could get the spirit "baptism" he would thus be secure. He became upset because a good Baptist friend did not have "tongues" but had the real assurance of his salvation.

As a high schooler, he had great conflicts and determined to go to Hollywood and become an actor. Having seen at least one pastor dismissed for immorality, he had come to hate preachers. He also loathed the idea of having to be identified with the "Holy Roller" church.

While attending a northern university, the Lord again dealt with him about giving his life to Christian service. He made up his mind to do so, but ended up in a Pentecostal Bible school. Here he became involved in midnight prayer meetings with other young men who were seeking the "baptism" of the Spirit. They kept urging him on. There was much praying, some were having visions, others were "dancing in the spirit."

Brooks was very sincere, and once while lying prostrate before the Lord he received something which he believes now was akin to the flooding of love experienced by Charles G. Finney. Never had he had such peace and joy. He was filled with the Spirit of God. Of this he was sure. But still no tongues! To please his friends and satisfy his professor, he attempted to imitate the gibberish he heard them uttering. He "let his speech organs wobble," tried giving himself over to the experience and all the rest, but he never spoke in tongues.

In the course of his work at the Bible school, he had to preach a sermon to the student body. He brought a message on the Spirit-filled life, and the chapel was very quiet that day. Since he did not have the "gift of tongues" they would not make a "minister" of him but only a licensed "worker."

The young man had begun to have serious doubts about some of the Assemblies Bible school leaders and teachers. He saw hardness and even cruelty on the part of those who were supposed to be sanctified. When he was called on for prayer, it bothered him that he could not pray because of the noise and confusion. He went out into the field to do home mission work for a year. Having serious conflicts, he began to study the Bible on his own. He soon began to see and believe some Bible truths he had never understood before.

First, he learned that the Bible taught the eternal security of the blood-bought believer in Christ. He began to feel that sixty to seventy percent of the tongues people he had known were seeking *security,* if they only knew it. The other thirty to forty percent he felt were sincerely seeking a deeper life with the Lord.

Second, he saw that the Bible nowhere taught that we were to seek any "baptism of the spirit."

Third, he learned that tongues were definitely not for all, according to the Bible. He saw that they were building supposition upon supposition.

Fourth, he saw that people were seeking this experience of practicing tongues almost like an automaton. Many times they were thinking of something else entirely. Like the young woman whom he saw get up from the altar after having tarried there for an hour or more past church time. Her baby was crying back at her seat, obviously wet, cold and hungry after being in church for three hours. The mother came back to the baby, shook him good, said "shut up!" and went back to seek her "tongues." A marked absence of love was noted.

Though some of his teachers were good, sincere, Christian men, and though they even used much sound material in this Pentecostal school, he grew less and less enamored with the Pentecostal movement. Finally his decision was made—he must make the break. This he soon did.

Peter Brooks was greatly relieved, he said, to be away from the false piety and away from the hierarchy of the movement. He traveled to an Assemblies of God conference to announce his withdrawal. There he had to face a dear uncle who was a veteran minister in the movement. He announced that he was going to have to leave the Assemblies, explaining that he had learned that tongues could be easily imitated and that the timing of the tongues-speaking and the "interpretations" often were absurd. His uncle replied, "What you are saying is true, but believe it anyway!"

Several other disillusioned students left the tongues movement at the same time. Peter Brooks joined a Bible church and later a Baptist church. He is now a gifted and much-used missionary, flying, evangelizing, singing, teaching and establishing churches under Baptist Mid-Missions in northeast Brazil. I had the joy of interviewing him while he was on furlough in Dayton, Tennessee, in December, 1974.

The thing that impressed me most was this: It was the ACTUAL Spirit-filled life, with its attendant knowledge of the Bible, that led him AWAY from the (counterfeit) tongues movement!

As this godly missionary looks back on his experience with "tongues," he lists the following EVIL EFFECTS of it:

1. Tongues became a substitute for Christ Himself.

2. The tongues people were depending on their emotions for security.

3. They felt that they were a "closed society," thus better than other Christians who had not attained to "tongues."

4. Spiritual growth was stunted by the movement. They indeed received "new insight" but not the correct insight.

5. Though they claimed to be "holy," it was the bickering of these "saints" that soured him on the whole thing.

Chapter 6

THE TANGLE
OVER TONGUES

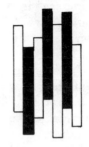

God is not the author of confusion," God assures us in I Corinthians 14:33. Yet much confusion abounds today in the tangle over tongues. To hear the 700 Club testimonies and to read the Full Gospel magazines, you would assume that this is the most exciting and helpful experience that a man could ever have.

A charismatic evangelist, introduced by a Pentecostal pastor on a telecast in Panama City, Florida, called this "baptism of the Spirit" the "main focal point of the teaching of Christ," and declared that all Christians should have these gifts. But he did not tell us that Christ never spoke in tongues nor even once advocated it. In referring to Paul's letter to the Corinthians, he did not tell us that it was a corrective letter to the most carnal church of all.

As these Pentecostals continued their "tongues" dialogue, they did not do us the service of telling the audience what the gift of "tongues" in Acts 2 really was. They carefully omitted what Paul actually said to discourage tongues in I Corinthians, and they did not tell us that Paul's first letter to Corinth was the *only* letter among all of them written to the churches in which this "experience" was even mentioned. The man claimed to be an evangelist, but he did not inform us that the great evangelists of all time (Wesley, Whitefield, Moody, Finney, Billy Sunday—to name a few) did not believe in nor practice "tongues." They did not tell us that the modern tongues movement actually began since 1900. Yet we were to believe that it was "the main focal point of the teaching of Christ"!

In a big church page ad before me, the "Johnnie Robinson Charismatic Crusade" announces "six glorious days" in Panama City. The evangelist promises to NAME the man of sin "who is alive in the world today and show pictures of the Antichrist and the castle in which he lives." This is interesting in view of the fact that the Bible tells us the Antichrist will not be revealed until after Christ comes for His own (II Thessalonians 2:3,8). The charismatic, in announcing his "miracle services," put himself in the place of Christ by stating that "no man could do such things except God be with him," and quotes a local pastor as saying, "When Johnnie prays, sin and sickness have to go!" Then we were modestly informed that none other than healer-turned-Methodist

Oral Roberts says, "Without question, Johnnie is one of the best." To top it off, Johnnie himself humbly asserts, "Jesus came to me IN PERSON [how wonderful!—capitals mine] and breathed faith into my heart until I cannot doubt God. I have the substance of that which you have been hoping for. Your hour of deliverance has come!" So there you have it.

A Rocky Mount, North Carolina, Church of God pastor put a large ad in the *Rocky Mount Evening Telegram* to attempt to reply to a local news editorial stating that tongues are being overemphasized. The Pentecostal pastor quotes John 14:16, where Christ promises to give another Comforter, as He indeed does, but that promise of the Comforter says nothing at all about tongues, nor are they implied. He then quotes Acts 2:39, but does not clarify the preceding verse which simply tells us that true believers receive the Holy Spirit without once mentioning tongues. To try to prove that tongues have not ceased nor knowledge vanished away, he refers to the knowledge that men have to go to the moon. Thus the pastor reveals that he does not know the difference between the revelatory, divine knowledge which God gave to holy men before the Bible was completed and the carnal, scientific knowledge of unsaved men in their space ventures today!

The North Carolina brother states, "As far as tongues not being for us today, this is the natural evidence of the baptism of the Holy Ghost." Yet the Bible does not once state that "speaking in tongues" is an evidence of being

Spirit-filled nor that any Christian is ever commanded to seek this experience. He quotes from I Corinthians 14:4 as if to teach that tongues are given by God to edify the Christian, when what Paul is really doing here is rebuking the carnal Corinthians for their Christian selfishness in edifying themselves instead of being concerned about doing something to edify the church. The entire ad shows the gross ignorance of those who do not "rightly divide the word of truth."

Two California medical doctors were deceived by the movement. They had gone to Denver where they spoke in tongues. Upon their return home, according to Dr. J. Vernon McGee (*Talking in Tongues,* Part 2, page 24), they began to examine themselves. Finally, in one of their homes, they were down on their knees praying. One of them said, "The Spirit of God has spoken to my heart that this is not of God." The other doctor said, "I have just been waiting for you to say it; I have felt that a long time. This is not of God." These two doctors got out of the tongues movement.

The movement is supposed to be spiritual and scriptural, yet Catholic Pentecostals testify that the charismatic experience has deepened their devotion to Mary. Stanley Gundry of Moody Bible Institute writes, "Catholic charismatic leaders and members of the hierarchy are appealing to the movement to remain in the Roman church and 'to remain faithful to the leadership of the papacy.'"

Thus people may have this "gift" while practicing the sacrifice of the mass, penance, and

Mariolatry, and while believing in papal infallibility, the authority of the Roman church and the traditions of Rome alongside the Bible—all further contributing to the tangle over tongues.

Wayne A. Robinson is the son of a Pentecostal preacher and is an author-minister-journalist and former Vice President of the Oral Roberts Evangelistic Association and Oral Roberts University. He has been a Pentecostal evangelist and a Methodist pastor. In this book, *I Once Spoke in Tongues,* he discusses his successful search for the "tongues" experience, only to ask himself if tongues had strengthened his preaching in any way or helped him win a single convert? After that, a Baptist preacher on a bus completely dumbfounded him with such simple questions as, "Where does it say in the Bible that speaking in tongues is the evidence of having received the baptism of the Holy Spirit?" and after quoting Acts 2:38, "What do *you* say they received?" He was thus brought face to face with the fact that the Bible did not say that the three thousand saved on Pentecost spoke in tongues at all; yet the Bible said they *did* receive the gift of the Holy Ghost! After that, Robinson began to study I Corinthians to see what Paul actually taught about tongues and found that Paul deliberately did *play down* the importance of tongues. In every list of the gifts of the Spirit, he put tongues last!

Charismatics at that time were encouraging Wayne Robinson to speak in tongues at will and often. He said, "I tried it and it worked. I could talk in tongues as easily as I could articulate the English language. The voluntary control was quite exciting. This was a new dimension and it bolstered my sagging enthusiasm." But when he practiced "tongues" during the day and for thirty minutes before speaking in meetings at night, he said nothing was helped by the tongues. "In fact," he said, "the edge of expectation which I usually experienced before speaking was dulled." Then Robinson said, "This all-out practicing of tongues convinced me that not only was it as easy to talk in tongues as it was to speak in English—the *feeling* was the same. The satisfaction was not even on a par with that gained by everyday conversation. It was not a religious feeling nor an emotional one; it was simply air being pushed through the larynx."

Midst the tangle over tongues, there are some who insist that the practice must come directly from the Holy Spirit, but Wayne Robinson asserts that many in the charismatic movement speak in tongues at will: "I know a minister who claims to speak in tongues while he is driving his car or shaving. He and others do not wait for a special time or place. They, and not God, initiate the speaking. They force the air from their lungs through their voice box. Though some tongues recipients may exhibit compulsive behavior, their habits do not arise out of their tongues speaking; their emotional patterns would be present whether or not they spoke in tongues."

Robinson has today discontinued the practice of tongues.

"God is not the author of confusion" (I Corinthians 14:33), yet many declare that the Full Gospel meetings inspire people to cause confusion and division in their churches. Churches are being split over tongues. Others are being captured by the charismatics. While the advocates of "tongues" act as if it was "the main focal point" of Christianity, the soul winners I have known who are most used of God had nothing to do with the idea.

Aside from the Pentecostal-type churches, it seems that this movement has developed most and fastest among churches that had already departed from the faith once delivered to the saints. Cold, formal, liturgical churches or worldly, carnal churches that are looking for some exciting new thing to stimulate the flesh seem to be the best soil for the movement to grow in. There are emotional people in all churches who long for something with a little "feeling" in it. This has not been provided by most modernistic churches in the past few years. The charismatic movement promises a new "high" for these folk.

Another obvious paradox that appears in the tangle over tongues is that women are very prominent in the movement. Yet the Bible expressly commands, in discussing tongues in I Corinthians 14:34, that the women were to be silent. There is no Bible proof that the Spirit of God ever inspired a woman to speak in a miraculous tongue. If then, women in Corinth were "speaking in tongues," as obviously they were, then whatever they had was not of God. Since our charismatic friends claim to receive the authority for their actions from Acts and I Corinthians, one wonders how they can sanction the participation of women in their "tongues speaking" today!

Well, perhaps we can soon untangle the tangle.

Chapter 7

ALL THAT GLITTERS IS NOT GOLD!

We have seen witch doctors speaking in tongues and singing in tongues (uttering unintelligible words) in their heathen ceremonies." So writes Missionary Alex R. Hay in his excellent book, *What is Wrong in the Church?* This discerning writer continues:

There is a Mohammedan sect that speaks in tongues. It is simply the result of an emotional state that is not normal and not difficult to induce. The fact is that "the gift of tongues," as it is known today, is still a common characteristic of primitive religions. (We refer to speaking in an unknown or "heavenly" language, unintelligible to the hearers, not the speaking of living languages that appeared at Pentecost.) As a child of missionary parents in an Indian tribe in Paraguay, we were accustomed to hear the witch doctors chanting in an unknown spirit language at their religious ceremonies or when treating someone who was ill.

Some of his amazing accounts of what happened there are startling and revealing indeed!

Since usually the phenomena of "tongues" and "faith healing" go hand in hand with their devotees, it would be interesting here to read Missionary Hay's conclusion about these "healers." He writes:

The results obtained by such faith healers are no more and no less than those obtained by healers in heathen religions and false cults, whose manner of playing upon the emotions is fundamentally the same. The witch doctor skillfully applies the same psychology to his patients with, as we have often personally witnessed, results that are certainly not inferior to those of many a "faith healer." And the maladies that the witch doctor is unable to cure are just those that the faith healer cannot cure!

In another chapter in this book on "counterfeit speaking in tongues," which every Christian should have and read, he states:

There is a significant similarity between the modern, so-called manifestation of unknown tongues and its manifestation in heathen religions. They are of exactly the same nature, produced by the same means. The effect upon the heathen worshipers is very much the same as is seen in so-called Pentecostal meetings. Emotions are given full sway. Religious fervor rises to a great height. There may be cries, groans, bodily contortions, ecstatic gesticulations, swooning. All of it is attributed to the presence of spirits. Behavior that would be considered undignified or improper at any other time is justified on the same ground. The moment the ceremony is over, those who have participated in it with such emotional abandon snap back to normal and will stand around and chat or resume their normal occupations as if nothing unusual had happened. They had participated in a religious act and now it is over.

Again:

That evil spirits take advantage of the error and extravagances in "Pentecostalism" is very evident. A very intelligent woman in one of our congregations in Brazil had been a spiritist medium before her conversion. Shortly after her conversion she moved to a city in which we did not have a church and she began to attend a "Pentecostal" congregation.

Briefly, she was told that she needed "the baptism of the Spirit" and "tongues" and the congregation began to pray that she would get it. During a prayer session filled with much emotion, she had a strange sensation as if she were rising into the air. She realized it was the same sensation she had felt as a spiritist medium and was in contact with evil spirits! She felt herself to be in danger, hurriedly left the meeting, and did not return.

A Spiritist medium in Brazil sometimes attended the Pentecostal meetings and explained why by saying, "I find it easy to communicate with the spirits in these meetings."

Yes, all that glitters in the religious realm is not gold.

Pentecostal pastors and other "tongues speakers" in Argentina were found to be keeping women for immoral practices or "tipsy" with drink while still practicing their supposed "gifts of the Spirit." "These were not rare exceptions, but examples of what is a common condition among the Pentecostal churches," Missionary Hay states.

Since error in doctrine and careless living are apt to go hand in hand, this could account for the Pentecostals in this country tolerating the long-haired male musicians, the raucous "gospel rock" music, so-called, and "testimonies" from charismatic night clubbers, right along with their Catholic, liberal, and Jesus freak groups of "tongues speakers."

Entertainer Pat Boone is quoted as saying, "When I run out of English and find myself groping self-consciously for the way to express myself, now I find complete freedom as the Holy Spirit, in this unfettered, infinitely expressive prayer language helps me to communicate directly with my Heavenly Father." At the last report Boone was still keeping his appointments in the liquor-saturated and licentious atmosphere of the night club circuit.

Though Oral Roberts left the Pentecostal people who had supported his meetings for years and joined the liberal Methodists, they still revere him as a great charismatic leader.

Out of curiosity, I once attended an Oral Roberts crusade in Mobile, Alabama. The music was pretty wild and jumpy even in those days. (Today his religious singers swish and sway to the rhythms of the world on his telecasts as he takes the most precious of sacred songs and perverts them to the beat of the same world that crucified our Lord.) The atmosphere was charged with the worked-up emotionalism of the affair. When Roberts appeared amid the greatly increased volume of the organ, with the spotlights on him, then began the screams and cries of arm-waving devotees as they stood to their feet for the grand entrance. By the end of the message, the hand-waving, tongues-talking and other outbursts were of such nature that my wife and I slipped out of the big tent, relieved to escape the atmosphere of that tent. It was time for the "healing" miracles, and I recalled again that Christ put out those who were wailing and making a noise when it was time for His (genuine) miracles (Luke 8:54).

A report of the Full Gospel Business Men's Fellowship World Convention meeting in Anaheim, California, in the fall of 1975, tells how the "big three" of the charismatic movement—Kathryn Kuhlman, Oral Roberts and Rex Humbard—helped bring large crowds with overflow audiences to the convention. As related in *The Baptist Challenge,* Oral Roberts, at the end of his message, sought to teach people to speak in tongues. Here were his exact words: "I'm going to quietly pray in tongues and when I give you the signal, you who already have the Holy Spirit, you very quietly start praying in tongues. And you that have never prayed in tongues, you join—and don't pray in English. Pray only with your heart. Don't let the words come out of your head. Pray only what comes up from your spirit."

One woman started screaming and wailing but her screams were soon lost in the "tongues praying" in unison. Then as Roberts quickly left, the FGBMFI men began their nightly ministry of trying to help people receive the "baptism of the Holy Spirit," and seeing them "slain in the spirit." It was not uncommon to see 12 to 15 people lying on the floor following their "experience."

Writer Kurt Koch tells of eighteen Japanese churches ruined and destroyed by the entrance of the "tongues" movement. In still another country, Dr. Koch had a young girl student come to him greatly disturbed because one of the teachers in that school was a follower of the new tongues movement and had dragged a number of the students into the same experience. On top of this, the woman had lesbian tendencies and had committed sexual offenses with some of the girl students. Yes, laxity of doctrine and morals may well go together.

Pastor David Cummins of Colonial Hills Baptist Church, Atlanta, Georgia, brought to his people an excellent series on this subject. I remember that he told of a former missionary to China who attended a Chinese Pentecostal service. Hearing an associate speaking and shouting under some unusual power in excellent Chinese and not wanting to be left out of the blessing, he let his mind become quite blank and began yielding himself to some external power. Then he began to feel a paralysis and numbness in his feet. Next, it affected his legs and he knew he would soon be prostrate on the floor. Then the numbness reached his knees. "I became alarmed," he said. "This thing was not coming upon me from Heaven but from beneath. This is the wrong direction!" He prayed, "May the blood of Christ protect me from this thing!" At once it vanished and he was normal again. Later, his co-worker, much sobered and chastened, said to him, "Ray, the thing that happened to me that night wasn't of God. It was of the devil." Then he described the spiritual darkness into which he was plunged following that ecstatic experience.

Truly, not all that glitters with religious excitement is gold.

But, some point to John L. Sherrill and other charismatics who say they did make an honest investigation and found "tongues" to be the real article. What about that? I have read a number of these books and articles. Think with me a moment.

Sherrill had found out that he had cancer and must undergo surgery. He admittedly was afraid. Then he was encouraged by friends to believe, but in his book he says nothing about repentance and/or relying upon the blood of Christ for salvation and redemption. It was simply "a leap of faith" he called it, saying, "All right; I believe Christ was God." Now every true Christian must believe that Christ was God all right, but that is not all one must believe. ("The devils also believe that, and tremble," the Scripture asserts in James 2:19!) His self-consciousness and ego seemed to go and he was relaxed as he went into surgery.

Now this is fine, and he may truly have received Christ and been born again, but I couldn't find that he said so! And, since following that experience, his religious contacts were with liberals and neo-evangelicals (Mrs. Ruth Peale, Dr. Van Dussen of Union Seminary, and dyed-in-the-wool tongues-speaking charismatics), there was nothing to reveal that anyone ever did tell him how to be saved.

A young Reformed church pastor told him of a desired tongues experience which he said the Bible calls "the baptism in the Holy Spirit." He spoke of the "wave of warmth" that swept down through his body when a charismatic put her hands upon his head and prayed in tongues. (But we have seen from the above episodes on the mission fields that this could have been *any* kind of spirit causing a "wave of warmth.") He received favorable words from noted modernists affiliated with the National Council of Churches and from Catholic leaders. He discovered from investigation that the Mormons and other false cults had engaged in "tongues speaking." But none of his spiritual help came from sound Christians of orthodox persuasion, as far as the record goes.

A successful businessman who began to speak in "tongues" was told that he was speaking "Chinese." Believing this, he gave up his lucrative business and decided to go to China with the gospel, but over in China he found, to his dismay, that he was only making unintelligible sounds!

Alex Hay reports that when studies were made with a group of former Pentecostals, it was discovered that they were finding it difficult to recover from the harmful effect that those years of emotional excesses had had on their nervous systems. They told of some who had ended up in mental institutions. As Mr. Hay spoke to them, he noticed the tendency to emotionalism, the faces twitching, the breathing quickening, and several times he had to speak so as to restore calmness.

A dentist who was a member of Pastor Hay's church in Paraguay had studied mesmerism in dental school. One of his professors practiced it and could so mesmerize a patient that he could not feel the extraction of a tooth. The dentist had come out of a Pentecostal church because he became convinced that the methods they use to influence people and get results is simply mesmerism and not the Spirit of God at all.

A Catholic student, disenchanted with the Catholic church, attended a Pentecostal meeting, searching for reality. When told to seek the gift of "tongues," he deliberately said a few words in Latin. The Pentecostals were delighted and told him he had spoken in tongues and they would interpret. However, their "interpretation" was not what he had said at all, and his test was over!

A. A. Allen, a noted charismatic "healer" who came from the same healing, tent-meeting era as Jack Coe and Oral Roberts, was found dead in his hotel room in San Francisco in June of 1970. The coroner said he died of acute alcoholism and fatty infiltration of the liver. The healer had come to the city for an operation on his arthritic knee. Yes, healers die, too, despite their tongues and "healing miracles" on others.

Dr. Koch writes:

> The tongues movement is an epidemic which rages over disturbed humanity. An indication of this is that heathen and Christians, possessed people and tribal dancers, witch doctors and spiritists can all speak in tongues. It is an expression of a delirious condition through which a breaking in of demonic powers manifests itself (I Timothy 4:1).

Some of the discussions and testimonies on the 700 Club and other charismatic broadcasts appear so shallow and absurd as to be ludicrous if they did not involve precious souls. In their endless chatter, they rattle on and on, and often nothing has really been said.

One woman was rejoicing that her cat had been healed in answer to prayer. In a written article, the story was told of a praying parakeet! Sometimes they get a businessman who doesn't know much about the Bible to tell about his charismatic experience. When they can get a compromising evangelist or a deceived pastor from among the Baptists or some Protestant denomination, they have scored a direct hit.

Dave Wilkerson, well-known minister to addicts, states, "Tongues takes the place of narcotics for many former addicts." For many charismatics, tongues is a "spiritual high"—emotional, but certainly not spiritual.

A charismatic in New York state claims to have the gift of discernment, boasting that he can tell if a saved person walked into the room. His discernment consists of a weird feeling in his scalp that goes down his back and makes his toes tingle. Then he asks them if they're saved, and every time they say they are!

Television and movie actor Marjoe Gortner was ordained to preach at the age of four and was billed as a boy wonder on the miracle-preaching circuit. He preached for years. Women would swoon and fall to the floor at his touch and his command. He says now that he was just *acting,* and that while he could have made a lot of money in the healing-revival business, he became bitter about it all by the time he had reached seventeen, and realized what his mother had done to him. Yet great crowds had faith in his power to heal by the "laying on of hands." Marjoe laughs about it all and says it was all psychosomatic.

So truly, that which glitters in the religious arena may be anything but gold!

Recent comers to charismatic belief who insist, on the basis of Mark 16:17, that tongues speaking is genuine and for today should take just as seriously the mention of snakes in the following verse. In West Virginia on October 24, 1974, a snake-handler was buried after a foot-stomping funeral that featured an electric guitar and three wriggling rattlers. The corpse had been a snake-handler at holiness services the previous Sunday. He died Monday after refusing medical help. Others had died two months earlier.

In East Tennessee a year or so ago, some religious zealots died from handling rattlesnakes. They were determined to fulfill the verse which says, "In my name shall they cast out devils; they shall speak with new tongues; they shall take up serpents" (Mark 16:17,18). The tongues talking can be explained in various ways. But rattlesnakes are extremely hard to reason with!

Even so, it is certain that there are many dear and sincere Christians among the holiness and Pentecostal folk who have not gone to such extremes and who are greatly embarrassed at what many of the new breed of worldly, ecumenical charismatics are doing to their cause. But let us continue our search for the truth about tongues. Please remember to "try the spirits whether they are of God" (I John 4:1).

Chapter 8

HOW TO SPEAK IN TONGUES

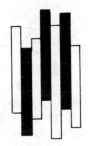

First, you'd better make sure that you really *want* to know how to speak in tongues. Wayne A. Robinson tells of Pentecostal students in Texas who "got started and couldn't stop" speaking in tongues. They obviously found themselves under the control of something they hadn't reckoned on.

In describing his attainment of the tongues experience, John Sherrill in *They Speak With Other Tongues* says: "Slowly I began to lose my own identity, too.... This is quite an experience, losing consciousness of self. And I was helped by gaining, at the same time, the awareness that another presence was in the room... the light blazed through my closed lids, blinding, dizzying, fearful. I was afraid of this approaching contact...." He continued to tell how the other charismatics gathered around him in the room singing, praying, encouraging—until finally he was pouring forth a torrent of "joyful sounds."

"Speaking in tongues is a venture of faith," writes Larry Christenson in his *Speaking in Tongues* book. "You lay aside any language you have ever learned, then lift up your voice and speak out. The risk is that you will say nothing more than bla-bla-bla. But when you take this step of simple faith, you discover that God indeed keeps His side of the bargain, and begins to shape the sound which you continue to give Him into a language of prayer and praise."

In his later advice about how to speak, he continues, "Focus your thoughts on Christ. Then simply lift up your voice and speak out confidently. . . . Take no particular thought of what you are saying, for your *mind is 'unfruitful'* during the exercise of this gift. As far as you are concerned, it will be just a series of sounds," etc., etc.

Wayne Robinson in *I Once Spoke in Tongues,* describes a tongues-speaking pastor instructing a lady who wanted the gift: "Do you remember when you were a little girl you used to say, 'Peter Piper picked a peck of pickled peppers; a peck of pickled peppers Peter Piper picked?' "

"Yes, I do," she replied. "But I always had trouble saying it. I would get the words mixed up."

"Exactly!" he exclaimed. "Now I'm going to tell you some words just like that. I want you to repeat them after me. You will get them mixed up, too, but don't worry about it. Keep saying them over and over, and soon you will be speaking in tongues. O.K.?"

Then she followed him around the room and repeated these words verbatim: "Blessed Jesus, suffering Saviour, save the sin-sick souls of sinful sinners. We wait willingly, wantingly, wonderfully, wistfully, right now!" Faster and then slower, and then faster she repeated the words as he led the pace. Soon she was standing with her arms outstretched and tears streaming down her face while she repeated strange sounds. The watching group was told that she had thus been filled with the Spirit. What they heard, he said, was talking in tongues.

A St. Louis Lutheran clergyman told his trainees for tongues, "Open your mouth as wide as possible and say 'Jesus—Jesus—Jesus—Jesus,' increasing your speed until you accomplish the act."

"Abadaba avadaba rehbadaba ramanama" were the words uttered by one man as another laid his hands gently on the top of his head and another took the left and right side of his jaw in the thumb and first finger of each hand, saying, "Now pray, Jim, say whatever the Lord gives you to say, and I will move your mouth" (From the book, *The Psychology of Speaking in Tongues* by John R. Kildahl).

I must confess I never knew how close I was to a traumatic religious experience when, as a child, I used to play "aba daba" and recite "Peter Piper picked a peck of pickled peppers!"

Remember, as Rev. John Ashbrook tells us,

in the tongues meetings you find the repetition of "Jesus, Jesus," or "Glory, glory, glory," or the chanting of "Blessed Jesus, Blessed Jesus." No one ever learned this routine from the Scriptures. I am reminded that Jesus Himself condemned "vain repetitions, as the heathen do" (Matthew 6:7). Pastor Ashbrook continues, "The phenomenon is almost like an emotional drug habit. Once a person has supposedly had it they are let down and must seek it again and again to keep up." He describes people he counseled with whose minds had begun to crack under the strain, but when they ceased to be exercised about tongues, normalcy returned.

I was once attending a revival crusade in west Florida where a noted Jewish evangelist was preaching. The word was going forth in power. Conviction was great. Suddenly a woman arose and began waving her arms and jerking her head. She began to cry out in a gibberish of "tongues." You could feel the power of the devil as the Bible message was interrupted. The evangelist called for the ushers to take her out of the meeting, stopping just long enough in his sermon to say, "The Holy Spirit doesn't do business that way!" You could feel the change of atmosphere after the offending woman was removed from the building. God again began to move on hearts that night and souls were saved.

In a Texas city, Dr. Louis Entzminger was preaching the gospel. Some tongues-speaking women began to attend and would interrupt his preaching with their messages and interpretations. He decided to put them to a test.

He persuaded a Greek restaurant owner, who was a Christian, to attend with him and to stand in the early part of the service and utter a paragraph from the Bible in Greek. When the Greek had finished his "discourse" in beautiful, pure Greek, the women began to wave their arms and declare they had an "interpretation." What they said bore no resemblance at all to what the Greek Christian had been saying. Dr. Entzminger then called his friend to the platform and had him repeat the Scripture in English which had been his "tongue" in Greek a few minutes before. The "tongues-speaking" women slunk away from the meeting and never returned.

A young wife in Florida learned to speak in tongues, she said, but lost her home and her husband. A fine missionary couple found "great new joy" in the charismatic movement, but many fruitful years on the mission field where once they won so many souls have been lost while they are experiencing this "charisma."

A preacher was in the habit of praying in tongues before giving his message. It now happens that sometimes he cannot cease from speaking in this "tongue" and has to have a towel given him to stop up his mouth. Dr. Koch asks, "What powers are these if the preacher cannot end his own prayers?"

Donald Burdick in his Moody Press publication, *Tongues, to Speak or Not to Speak,* says, "It seems that the origin of most current glossolalia lies in the area of the psychological." He then deals with such topics as Ecstasy, Hypnosis, Psychic Catharsis, Breakthrough of the Unconscious and Exalted Memory. In quoting investigating psychiatrists, he describes how the "tongues speaker" combines sounds in new patterns because he has learned to be released from adult inhibitions and controls of the normal speech pattern. Included may be nonsense syllables, perhaps some foreign terms embedded in the subconscious, etc., and sometimes English words. The joy and peace comes because the glossalalic (tongues speaker) feels that his accomplishment is an evidence of God's acceptance and favor, the hallmark of spiritual attainment. Dr. Burdick concludes (capitals mine), "In reality, if the explanation above is reasonably consonant with the facts, THE EXPERIENCE OF GLOSSOLALIA IS ONE OF TEMPORARY ABNORMALITY. THE BRAIN IS NOT FUNCTIONING ACCORDING TO ITS NORMAL PATTERN, a kind of short circuit has been produced and the rational area has been temporarily blocked out of the mental network. . . ."

This being the case, I would not delve into tongues, nor attempt to get this "baptism" for one of the same reasons that I would not drink liquor. I have no brain to spare! One tongues leader said, "Is there anything more FUN than praising God?" But of course, the libertine can say the same thing about his fornication, and the drunk can say the same about his bottle.

Greek scholar Spiros Zodhiates, commenting on this, says, "Speaking with an unknown tongue by-passes intelligence. Beware of any action of the spirit that ignores the God-given faculty of thinking" (*Why Speak with Tongues,* Vol. 3). In Volume 4 of his excellent series, Dr. Zodhiates takes up the views of the linguists who have examined the recordings of such glossolalia, and states, "From the viewpoint of a Christian linguist, the modern phenomena of tongues would appear to be a linguistic fraud and monstrosity."

The title of this chapter, you'll remember, gentle reader, is "How to Speak in Tongues." But by now are you sure you want to try? Perhaps it will help us to the truth, to see in the next chapter, what the original gift of tongues really was.

Chapter 9

WHAT WAS THE REAL GIFT OF TONGUES?

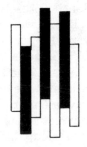

There is, in serious Bible study, what is called the Law of First Mention. Generally, the place where a truth is first discovered, you will find the key to the understanding of the passage. In other words, the key is in the front door! The matter of tongues is no exception.

The first mention of a New Testament experience of tongues is in Acts, chapter 2. The actual meaning of the word "tongues" (Greek, *glossa*) here is *languages*. There were at least sixteen different nationalities represented in Jerusalem that day when multitudes were congregated in the Holy City to commemorate the day of Pentecost. They are listed in verses 9 through 11, so that everyone can know that fact. We are told, in verse 10, that there were Jews and proselytes from these countries there. A proselyte was one who was a non-Jew but had accepted the Jewish religion and observed its laws and ceremonies just like a Jew. So Gentile proselytes were in Jerusalem on that

There were also Christians there. These were Jews who had accepted Jesus Christ as their Saviour. The disciples and other believers of Acts 1 who had met in the upper room were "all with one accord in one place" (Acts 2:1) in Jerusalem on the day of Pentecost. Ever since the resurrected Christ told them to stay in Jerusalem and wait for the promised Spirit who would come and empower them to be witnesses to all the world of Christ (Acts 1:4-8), this group of believers had continued with one accord together. On this Jewish Pentecost feast day, when the multitudes were filling the streets of Jerusalem, these Christians were sitting in a house, fellowshiping together. Nothing is said about going into a frenzy, a trance, or ecstatic entreaties while "tarrying" for the Spirit to come. They were just sitting in a house in sweet accord because of their love for Christ and in obedience to Him.

Then, in God's perfect timing, there suddenly came a sound from Heaven like a rushing mighty wind, and it filled all the house where they were sitting. There appeared unto them cloven tongues like as of fire—gleaming but neither burning nor being consumed—which sat upon each of them. And they were all filled with the Holy Spirit and began to speak with other tongues (languages), as the Spirit gave them utterance.

For some reason the charismatics today

never manage to simulate the rushing wind and the cloven tongues of fire sitting over each participant. If being "Pentecostal" means that this Pentecostal occurrence should be the experience of Christians today, it would be reasonable to assume that God could reproduce the entire episode.

Now we might not know what the "other tongues" of verse 4 were if the Lord did not make it plain in the next verses that there were dwelling at Jerusalem at that time Jews from every nation under heaven and a multitude of them came to see what was going on and "every man heard them speak in his own language." The people were amazed at this because the speakers were all Galileans, and Galileans were not known for their scholarly education. Yet, they said, "How hear we every man in our own tongue, wherein we were born?" After mentioning all the nationalities present as an expression of their amazement, they said again, "We do hear them speak in our tongues the wonderful works of God! What meaneth this?"

From this account, wouldn't it seem that almost any elementary school child would know that the gift of tongues that day at Pentecost was a miracle of real foreign languages? It was clearly a miracle produced by the Holy Spirit to allow these Christians to witness to people of "every nation under heaven." What was the result? Peter had the attention of multitudes and he preached to them Christ, and 3,000 souls were saved and baptized that day and added to the company of believers.

What was the purpose of the rushing mighty wind, the cloven tongues like as of fire, and the speaking with tongues? These were the magnificent manifestation of the coming of the Holy Spirit to take up permanent residence in these believers, the first members of the body of Christ, the church. Christ promised His followers that after He went away He would send them another Comforter, "the Spirit of truth," who would abide with them forever. The Holy Spirit would live in them and would teach them all things (John 14:16-26).

The coming of the Holy Spirit upon these believers was the beginning of a new era. The Spirit thus baptized these believers into the one body of Christ. The Apostle Paul explains it this way: "For by one Spirit are we all baptized into one body..." (I Corinthians 12:13). Christ promised that the Spirit would come for this purpose, and He came. This was an event never to be repeated.

But tongues are mentioned in two other places in the book of Acts. How can this be if the event of Acts 2 can never be repeated? The answer is there, in these other two places. Let us look at them. We should notice as we look that both times the expression is not "speaking in tongues," but, as in Acts 2, the expression is that "they spoke with tongues."

In Acts 10, in obedience to God, Peter preached the gospel to Cornelius and other Gentiles gathered with him in Caesarea: "To him [Jesus] give all the prophets witness, that through his name whosoever believeth in him shall receive remission of sins" (verse 43).

While Peter was still speaking, and to the surprise of the Jews who had come to Caesarea with him, the Holy Spirit fell on all them who heard the word.

Their surprise was not because the gift of the Holy Spirit was given, but because it was given also to the *Gentiles*—"for they heard them [Gentiles] speak with tongues, and magnify God" (verse 46). Peter's friends knew the Holy Spirit had come to take up permanent residence in the believing Jewish Christians on the day of Pentecost—but on *Gentiles*?

Earlier in the tenth chapter we are told that Peter had been prepared by God with the vision of the great sheet for taking the gospel to the Gentiles. He asked the surprised Jews, "Can any man forbid water, that these [Gentiles] should not be baptized, which have received the Holy Ghost as well as we?" (verse 47).

Yes, Peter and presumably his companions ("they of the circumcision who believed. . . as many as came with Peter?" (verse 45), had received the Holy Ghost on the day of Pentecost when He came upon all the existing believers—about 120 people (Acts 1:15). From that time on, as we learn from the epistles, the Spirit comes upon every new believer in Christ and baptizes him into the body of Christ. That is what happened here when Cornelius believed. See the sequence of events?

In Acts 10, Cornelius, a Roman soldier, that is, a Gentile, and a devout man, one who feared God and prayed to him, was given a vision by God. God was about to do a great thing. He was about to open the way for salvation to come to the Gentiles, for in this new organism, the body of Christ, there were to be both Jews and Gentiles. Cornelius was told to send to Joppa for Simon Peter (verse 5).

The next day, as Cornelius' three messengers were approaching Peter's house in Joppa, God gave Peter a vision while he was in prayer upon his housetop. The message that came to Peter through this vision was that what God cleansed should not be refused. While Peter was still puzzling over the meaning of the vision, behold, the messengers were at his gate asking him to go to the home of the Gentile, Cornelius. Peter was not left in doubt long, for the angel whispered in his ear, "Arise therefore, and get thee down, and go with them, doubting nothing: for I have sent them" (verse 29). Thus, Peter was divinely prepared for what was about to happen. He could then say, "Of a truth I perceive that God is no respecter of persons" (verse 34), and he preached Christ to Cornelius, that "whosoever believeth in him [Christ] shall receive remission of sins" (verse 43).

It took a divine manifestation to convince the Jews that a Gentile could be brought into the body of Christ, and so the Spirit's gift of "speaking with tongues" was poured out on Cornelius and he magnified God with languages that everyone around him could understand. There were evidently at least three different tongues spoken by those in Caesarea: Latin, Greek and Aramaic, and perhaps many more in that important Roman city.

In Acts 19 we read that the Apostle Paul

came to Ephesus and found there certain "disciples." Paul questioned these disciples. Perhaps they showed a lack of spirituality or power in their lives. He asked if they had received the Holy Spirit when they believed ("when," we are told, is the literal and better translation for "since" in verse 2).

Their answer revealed that they were disciples or followers of John the Baptist and had been baptized with John's baptism, looking forward, like Old Testament saints, to the coming of the Messiah, Christ the King. When they heard that Christ had already come (and undoubtedly Paul told them the full gospel story, that Christ had died for the sins of the world, was resurrected and had returned to the Father), they were baptized in the name of Christ, showing they believed on Him as Saviour. Then the Holy Spirit came upon them, and they spoke with tongues and prophesied (verses 5,6).

These disciples of John the Baptist rejoiced in their new faith in the Lord Jesus Christ and praised God with foreign languages they did not know but which could be understood by those present. Ephesus was a cosmopolitan city and many languages were spoken there.

Obviously the coming of the Holy Spirit on the day of Pentecost in Acts two and the two events in chapter 10 and 19 of Acts were all a part of the coming of the Holy Spirit to initiate believers into the body of Christ.

(1) He came to the Jewish believers at Pentecost, and to authenticate the occasion, He

gave them the sign of speaking with other tongues as 3,000 souls were brought to a knowledge of Christ.

(2) He came to Cornelius as the first of the Gentiles to become a part of the body of Christ, to authenticate this occasion to the Jews. There is no reason for this sign to be repeated. All other Gentiles who believed on Christ after that were evidently saved without the manifestation of this sign. Once was sufficient. The Philippian jailer, for example—apparently a Gentile—did not speak with other tongues (Acts 16:30-34). But he gave evidence of his salvation by his deeds, as we all should.

(3) He came to John the Baptist's former disciples with the same sign of speaking with other tongues to show the Jews that those who believed under the Old Testament era (under John the Baptist's teaching, for instance) needed also to become a part of this new organism, the body of Christ. There are no Old Testament saints living today, are there? Therefore, there is no reason for the sign of tongues to be repeated for this purpose!

Once we understand the purpose of this coming of the Holy Spirit with the sign of speaking with tongues, we need never again be confused about whether we Christians today "might be missing something" by not speaking in a babbling of tongues or with tongues we have never learned. The sign of speaking with tongues was to the Jews to show them that God was initiating something new.

If we honestly search the New Testament, we soon learn that God used certain signs given to the Jews ("For the Jews require a sign," I Corinthians 1:22) to authenticate the Word of God and God's dealings with men:

"Then said Jesus unto him, Except ye see *signs* and wonders, ye will not believe" (John 4:48).

"Ye men of Israel, hear these words; Jesus of Nazareth, a man approved of God among you by miracles and wonders and *signs,* which God did by him in the midst of you, as ye yourselves also know... Him... ye have taken..." (Acts 2:22,23).

"Truly the *signs* of an apostle were wrought among you in all patience, in *signs,* and wonders, and mighty deeds" (II Corinthians 12:12).

"How shall we escape, if we neglect so great salvation; which at the first began to be spoken by the Lord, and was confirmed unto us by them that heard him; God also bearing them witness both with *signs* and wonders, and with divers miracles, and gifts of the Holy Ghost, according to his own will?" (Hebrews 2:3,4).

Signs and wonders also sometimes authenticated God's works to the Gentiles. The Apostle Paul used signs for this purpose: "For I will not dare to speak of any of those things which Christ hath not wrought by me, to make the Gentiles obedient, by word and deed, Through mighty *signs* and wonders, by the power of the Spirit of God; so that from Jerusalem, and round about unto Illyricum, I have fully preached the gospel of Christ" (Romans 15:18,19).

That God confirmed His word with miraculous signs while the Book was still in the making, is evident. We read in Mark 16:17,18, "And these *signs* shall follow them that believe; In my name shall they cast out devils; they shall speak with new tongues; They shall take up serpents; and if they drink any deadly thing, it shall not hurt them; they shall lay hands on the sick, and they shall recover."

These verses give some people a lot of trouble. What do they mean? Should we look for these signs among believers today? Or were these signs fulfilled in Biblical history?

We have the fulfillment of the promise Christ made in this passage about new tongues in the "other tongues as the Spirit gave them utterance" in Acts 2:4, when the disciples miraculously spoke on Pentecost, and on the occasions recorded in Acts 10 and 19. In the ministry of Paul in Acts 16:18, we see the casting out of devils. And in Acts 28:1-6, we find the miraculous deliverance from the poisonous effects of a snake bite when Paul was accidentally bitten. In no case did God say they were to make a career out of speaking in new tongues or deliberately taking up serpents. Jesus said these were for "signs." As for laying hands on the sick and they shall recover, we have numerous instances in the days of the apostles when the sick were miraculously healed through their ministry. See Acts 3 for when Peter and John healed the lame man at the gate of the temple, and the healing of the father of Publius by Paul in Acts 28, as examples. Keep in mind that miracles are to Christianity what scaffolding is to a house—essential while under construction.

Remarkably, tongues is a subject never once mentioned to any other church in all the letters of the New Testament except to the carnal church, the Corinthians. Surely, if this sign-gift was important for all churches, it would have been dealt with often or at least mentioned to some of those great churches! This is highly significant!

Paul had to write to the church at Corinth to correct many spiritual and moral problems in the church. They also abused and misunderstood the gift of tongues. Paul uses three chapters of his first epistle to them (chapters 12 through 14) to deemphasize the importance of tongues and to regulate their use. Some gifts, he said, are temporary gifts, such as prophecy, knowledge, and tongues. "Charity never faileth: but whether there be prophecies, they shall fail; whether there be tongues, they shall cease; whether there be knowledge, it shall vanish away" (I Corinthians 13:8). They fulfill a temporary need until the Word of God is written in its entirety, and then they will end.

Keep in mind, then, that the word "tongues" in the Greek means traditional languages. It is used in the New Testament fifty times and is never used to teach some heavenly speech of ecstacy. The Bible says nothing about going into a frenzy, a trance, or an ecstasy to receive a "gift of tongues."

Out of sixty-six books in the Bible, only three of them mention tongues except one reference related to the Jews in the book of Isaiah. And where it is most mentioned, in I Corinthians, God through Paul is correcting and regulating. There are 1,189 chapters and 31,162 verses in the Bible, and only comparatively few verses deal with the subject in only seven chapters. All of this would surely indicate that it is hardly "the main focal point of the teaching of Christ," as some charismatics teach. In fact, Jesus Christ never commanded His followers to speak with other tongues!

Jesus plainly taught that the Holy Spirit was to come to give us power and that power was to make us effectual witnesses. Soul winning, then, is the great burden of God. "Ye shall be witnesses unto me after that the Holy Ghost is come upon you" (Acts 1:8).

Many good books of exposition have been written by scholars much more able than I about the gifts of the Spirit that are sovereignly given by God to believers that His work in the church might be accomplished. Some outstanding books of helps are listed at the end of this book for your further study, according to your interest. Enough evidence has been given here, I believe, to show the nature of the real gift of tongues.

Consider these thoughts in conclusion. Second Timothy 2:15 commands Christians to "study" their Bibles. To learn what you have read in this chapter requires diligent study. Babbling and emotional lather is, of course, easier than the hard work of honest Bible study.

The book of Acts is a transition book linking the age of the law and the earthly ministry of

Christ with the age of grace and the heavenly ministry of Christ.

Jameson, Fausett and Brown commentary says, "Tongues must mean languages, not ecstatic, unintelligible rhapsodies."

Never once were the disciples told to "lose themselves" to allow the take-over of their reason by some spirit, nor were they ever told to allow their speech organs to wobble and their minds to "become unfruitful," as some tongues people today say we should.

The Bible does *not* say that "speaking in tongues" is the initial evidence of the gift of the Holy Spirit to the believer.

In the Book of Acts the gift of languages was used three times only. Great numbers of new converts were made in chapters 2, 5, 8, and 9. The Bible does not even imply that they ever once spoke in tongues.

Chapter 10

REGULATING
THE RUMPUS

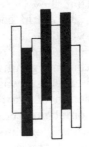

Are "tongues" for today and for everybody? And if not, where does the present charismatic confusion come from?

"Except ye see signs and wonders, ye will not believe," Jesus said in John 4:48, and surely He says it today to many who do not feel that the finished Word of God is enough revelation for them. Sadly, though, many today still "require a sign."

Tongues were not for everybody even back in the book of Acts. "Do all speak with tongues?" (I Corinthians 12:30), Paul asked, and the answer is self-evident. Certainly not! We have already learned that many of the converts in Acts did not exercise any such gift. At least there is no indication that they did. Jesus did not speak in tongues. Other Spirit-filled Christians did not—such saints as John the Baptist,

Elisabeth, Zacharias, Stephen, and Barnabas—though the Bible clearly reveals that they were filled with the Spirit.

It would seem quite clear that the gift of tongues, along with other sign-gifts were temporary. For one thing, there is no record that the genuine gift of spoken languages, as at Pentecost, was ever in effect again after the canon of Scripture was complete. False cults sometimes claimed a "gift of tongues," but where genuine revival and sound doctrine were found, there was no claim for a "tongues" gift. Charismatics today try to claim that they appeared during certain spiritual highs, but history does not substantiate this.

They have tried, for instance, to make us believe that "tongues" appeared during the great Welsh Revival of 1904, but actual letters and statements from that country and that era prove the claim untrue. Alex Hay, in his great book, *What is Wrong in the Church?* has some actual quotes on this from saints in Wales (page 103 in the book of that title, Vol. 2, subtitled "Counterfeit Speaking in Tongues").

Dr. John R. Rice, in his excellent booklet of radio messages entitled *Speaking in Tongues,* has described the false claims of the Full Gospel Businessmen's magazine in which they erroneously declare that D. L. Moody, Charles Finney and R. A. Torrey talked in tongues. Dr. Rice mentions a number of books by these great men which prove that they did not have any such "tongues" experience. These greatly used men of God did not believe in it. "Neither did Billy Sunday. I knew Billy Sunday. Neither did Gipsy Smith. Neither did Charles Finney," Dr. Rice asserts. Surely if these great men had been chasing around to "charismatic meetings" they would not have been the highly successful winners of multitudes of souls that they were!

During the time when the Corinthian letters were written, the sign-gifts may still have been in effect. There is reason to believe that they were. But while the gift of tongues (languages) was listed in I Corinthians 12, it is noteworthy that later in Ephesians 4:8-12 the gift of tongues was left out of the list. This is also true in Romans 12:4-8. When the fruit of the Spirit is so beautifully clustered in Galatians 5:22,23, there is no mention of tongues or other sign-gifts. In I Corinthians 13, Paul had told us that, along with (revelatory) knowledge and the gift of prophecy, "tongues shall cease" (I Corinthians 13:8) after the Scripture was complete. "That which is perfect is come" (I Corinthians 13:10) refers obviously to the completion of the perfectly revealed Word of God. "This adjective ('perfect') used as a noun is in the neuter gender. Therefore it is a reference to the finished (perfect) or completed Word of God. If it referred to Christ, it would be in the masculine gender" (William G. Bellshaw, Th. M.). This quote is taken from Dr. E. L. Bynum's very fine tract on tongues and charismatic renewal.

It is true that many godly men and students believe that the term "that which is perfect is come" refers to Christ coming, and to heaven, instead of to the completed and finished Word of God, because of the "now we see through a glass darkly; but then face to face" promise in verse 12 of I Corinthians 13. Still it seems significant to me that the phrase "tongues shall cease" occurs right between chapter 12 and chapter 14 where the tongues under discussion are being dealt with. Be that as it may, it is quite clear that the tongues of Acts 2 *did* cease after the canon of Scripture was completed since *this* sign-gift is never again mentioned in any of the other epistles to any church, nor is it listed among the gifts of the Spirit in later portions of the Bible (such as Ephesians 4 and Romans 12), nor mentioned as fruit of the Spirit in Galatians 5 or anywhere else in the Bible! Secular histories of the church bear out that the miraculous gift of tongues (foreign languages) was not found among sound preachers or missionaries in the centuries that followed. Of course, it is acknowledged that a sovereign God *could* give any gift He chose to at any time, but the contents of this book are surely enough proof that the modern tongues and charismatic chatter of today and the miraculous gift of Pentecost are not one and the same thing at all!

Evidently the Corinthians needed a lot of spiritual help. Paul was trying to regulate the rumpus in Corinth when he wrote I Corinthians 14. When Paul said, "I speak with *tongues* more than ye all" (I Corinthians 14:18), just keep in mind that the word means foreign *languages,* and there is no problem. He spoke a number of languages. Paul would have been glad for all of them to have so spoken in other languages (I Corinthians 14:5, the word "unknown" is not in the actual text), if they could have used their speaking to do intelligent "prophesying" or witnessing for the Lord. Keep in mind that Paul in I Corinthians 14 is correcting heresy. He is not telling them *how,* but how *NOT TO* speak in tongues!

The Corinthians were the most carnal of all the churches he addressed. They were *baby* Christians (I Corinthians 3:1-3), who refused to grow up and put away childish things; they went to law with one another to the dishonor of the Lord (I Corinthians 6); they had a first-class case of incest going on in the church (I Corinthians 5); they got drunk at the Lord's table (I Corinthians 11:21). Is it any wonder, then, that they got off into a tongues heresy (I Corinthians 14)?

Psychic phenomena were being experienced in Corinth. They had come to acknowledge the Lord out of a background of paganism where ecstatic and psychic tongues had been a part of their worship. It is little wonder that they now were confusing this with the genuine gift of Acts 2. Some may actually have been speaking foreign languages, but were doing so in disobedience. They were not to exercise the gift unless unsaved Jews were present (verses 21,22). They were to be sure and have an interpreter present (verses 27,28). There was to be no confusion (verse 33). The women were not to participate in tongues (verse 34). All things were to be done decently and in order (verse 40).

And evidently, some were simply putting on a show and were edifying themselves instead of the church (verse 4); they were not uttering words easy to be understood (verse 9); they were to grow up in the exercise of their gifts and stop being childish (verse 20); they were to use whatever gift they had for the unsaved instead of to tickle the fancy of believers (verse 22). Before the Bible was completed, and since they had no New Testament ("that which is perfect") to go by at that time, they listened to spiritual leaders (prophets) in the church who had a message, but they were to listen orderly and "by course" (verse 27), one holding his peace until the former had finished (verse 30). They were not to forsake their reason, become mentally "unfruitful" or let their voices wobble, but "the spirits of the prophets" were to be "subject to the prophets" (verse 32).

After the Corinthian correction, of course, tongues are never mentioned again. Perhaps they had learned their lesson by the time II Corinthians was written. Since sign gifts were soon to cease, the topic never comes up for discussion with any of the other churches: much less do we find any *command* to "speak in tongues." You see what a very simple thing it is to solve apparent problems of Scripture if we just "study. . . [and]. . . rightly divide the word of truth!"

Dr. B. F. Cate, in his excellent book, produced by the Regular Baptist Press, suggests that if *tongues* are still in effect, then "prophecy" must be too, and if that be the case, then we have no infallible Bible because these "prophets" are still getting divine truth for us. If this were the case, then we would not know whether we had a complete Bible or not! (*The Nine Gifts of the Spirit,* page 12).

Perhaps right here it would be good to remember that while "no *prophecy* of the scripture is of any private interpretation" (II Peter 1:20), the Bible only being *divinely* inspired, that "to *prophesy*" sometimes may mean to witness, to preach or to forth-tell. (See I Corinthians 14:1; Acts 2:18, etc.) Of course, all Christians should "prophesy" in this sense of witnessing and telling-forth the great mercies of the Lord. Remember, too, that while some who call themselves "divine healers" may be frauds, God *does* gloriously heal in answer to prayer (John 14:12-14; James 5:14-16) when it is His will to do so, and all Christians who live in fellowship with Him and meet His conditions have a right to claim these prayer promises! In fact, in the next chapter, you will discover that the peace and power of God can be ours, as believers, in this life as we allow the blessed Holy Spirit to have the right of way in our lives.

But, no wonder Paul had to regulate the rumpus at Corinth!

Now, what about the present rumpus of the charismatic movement?

Having read the previous chapters, you no doubt have ideas concerning the origins of "tongues," but let us contemplate a few possibilities.

Some are just imitating others like the "Peter Piper Picked a Peck" lady of Chapter 8. Some are self-hypnotized, like those who already have their minds made up to "fall under the power" at the healing meeting. Some are just fakes and later admit it, like the Greek restaurant owner who was playing a part, or Marjoe who admitted he was just acting. Some experience a breakthrough of the unconscious, while others experience so-called exalted memory and recall from the back recesses of the brain network some things from the past, as they allow their minds to become "unfruitful." And, according to some who have come out of the movement, a good bit of it may be demon-possession, or at least the activity of the devil to keep people from the "more excellent way."

Surely, anything that keeps sinners from salvation and keeps Christians from enjoying soul-winning power is of the evil one.

While many charismatics consider tongues "a *prestige* gift," to quote Dr. Lehman Strauss, exactly the opposite is true, according to Paul, who was trying to get these "baby" Corinthian Christians to put away their religious toys and grow up!

Sadly, the charismatic movement has come about partly because of the unreality in so many churches where there is an absence of life and power, and partly because of spiritual ignorance of the Bible. People who really understand the Bible will never get off into the "isms" and "wasms" and "spasms" of religious error.

While there are some sweet and sincere Christians among Pentecostals, they do not understand some of the blessed truths about the Holy Spirit and can never have great peace and assurance since they do not accept the glorious truth of the eternal security of the blood-bought believer.

I was recently with a dynamic young soul-winning pastor in a small Tennessee town. The Church of God movement (Pentecostal) is quite prominent there. It is a very difficult community to evangelize because so many think they were once saved and are now lost again. The pastor told me this doctrine has led a great many people off into sin, because they feel there is no use, that having been saved and lost it, they might as well give up and go on living in sin. This is sad, indeed. Though claiming to have this "gift of tongues" their missionaries, just like others, have to study for years to learn a language before serving on a foreign field.

People who are truly Spirit-filled will not be talking so much about their experience, or even about the Holy Spirit, as they will be exalting Christ (see John 16). We sing, "I would be like Jesus" in our churches. It is said that "*He* went about doing good," that He came to do the Father's will and "to finish His work," but never did He speak in tongues, either as an act of devotion to the Father or in order to give a sign to or communicate with men.

Why talk to God in an unknown or ecstatic tongue, when God understands English—or whatever language may be our own? Why use a supposed "tongue" to communicate with others if they understand our own "natural" tongue? Dr. Bob Jones used to say, "If it hasn't got any sense to it, then God isn't in it!"

To say that one is "Pentecostal" and then not

have the cyclonic wind, or the cloven tongues of fire sitting on him, or to be able to give the gospel to unsaved foreigners in their own language so that they can be saved, surely proves that one does not have the same thing experienced at Pentecost. Read Acts 2 again!

Since unsaved modernists and other Christ-denying infidels are in the charismatic tongues movement along with Mary-worshiping Roman Catholics, night club entertainers and other worldlings, we need to hear again the word of Paul to the Corinthians—and to all Christians today—when he says, "Be ye not unequally yoked together with unbelievers. . . . Come out from among them, and be ye separate, saith the Lord, and touch not the unclean thing; and I will receive you" (II Corinthians 6:14,17).

One noted evangelist has suggested that the charismatic tongues movement may be what Satan will use to get his world ecumenical church together. Certainly the charismatics and the ecumaniacs are traveling in the same direction now. It matters not what you believe as long as you have spoken in tongues.

The so-called charismatic renewal is anything *but* the real, spiritual revival our world so desperately needs.

Dr. J. B. Williams of Baptist Mid-Missions is a powerful preacher and has been a much-used missionary in darkest Africa. He has witnessed the heathen "tongues talking" on the mission field and the counterfeit charismatic "tongues" of this country. He says, "The tongues groups use only four to five sounds of the forty that can be made in English or the three hundred of which the human voice box is capable. It is impossible to communicate with only five sounds. Those interpreters are as phony as a lead nickel!"

Let us conclude this chapter with a variety of pertinent thoughts from various sources, keeping in mind that Paul warned of the Antichrist's activity in the days before the tribulation when "the mystery of iniquity doth already work" (II Thessalonians 2:7), and stated, concerning the work of the devil-incarnate, "Even him, whose coming is after the working of Satan with all power and *signs* and lying wonders" (II Thessalonians 2:9). We, then, can surely expect to find spurious "signs" and lying religious wonders in these days before the return of the Lord.

One man described his "tongues" experience by saying, "You just bubble, bubble." Doesn't that sound intelligent and spiritual?

A charismatic clinic is described in *Focus on Missions* with an Episcopal priest in charge. This one was in Alaska with an Episcopal priest and an Assemblies of God pastor speaking. A closed-circuit TV seminar was to bring teachings from David Wilkerson, Kathryn Kuhlman, Pat and Shirley Boone, and others. What a strange assortment of "religious" instructors!

Demos Shakarian, founder and president of the Full Gospel Businessmen's Fellowship, in an interview told how five students at Notre Dame went to a fellowship meeting at South Bend. They asked the chapter president to "baptize them in the Holy Spirit in his basement." "This was the beginning of the Roman Catholic tongues movement. It is interesting that a man can baptize anybody in the Holy Spirit—in his basement or anywhere else" (From *Focus on Missions*).

Paul Van Gorder writes:

> Bible doctrine is not established by what we experience. Rather, doctrine must determine the validity of the experience. This rule is frequently violated today. An example is a quote from a denominational committee report, "Be open to new ways in which God by His Spirit may be speaking to the church." Little wonder, then, that glossolalia, speaking in tongues, has been found in paganism, spiritualism, and occultism. Missionaries have witnessed this phenomenon, in this case not induced by the Spirit of God, but by evil spirits.

In viewing the entrance of Roman Catholics (formerly considered by the Pentecostal Holiness people as the epitome of evil, unbiblical religion) into the tongues movement, a Pentecostal leader has stated that the Pentecostal churches, "are having to make an agonizing reappraisal concerning what makes a Pentecostal." *Focus on Missions* comments: "What a strange position, indeed—to be a Pentecostal and yet not be sure what it takes to make one Pentecostal!"

Another writer says:

> Almost invariably, those who have experienced the so-called "baptism" have been

suffering from a very deep personal or family problem. They are looking for a way out. Others are emotionally troubled about their own spiritual lives. Quite a few drawn to the movement are emotionally high-keyed people. Some are mystics and visionaries. Some seek only experience to save them from the hard work of studying the Word of God. They want it easier.

For many of these people we trust that the last chapter of this book will be a help.

Dr. Earle E. Matteson, himself in the movement for a number of years and now a successful Baptist pastor in Denver, states: "If speaking in tongues is a sign of the baptism of the Spirit, then most Christians are not baptized by the Spirit. If a person is not baptized with the Spirit, then that individual is not saved (Romans 8:9). Also, the unbaptized person is not a member of the body of Christ, the church" (I Corinthians 12:13).

Dr. Matteson also reminds us that when three thousand were saved and baptized in water after the sermon at Pentecost, the same having received the Spirit (Acts 2:38), that "this would have been an excellent opportunity for God to set the pattern for the tongues movement. However, not one convert of the three thousand is indicated as speaking in tongues as a sign of his own baptism in the Spirit. Surely this would have been the moment to duplicate Pentecost. The Scriptures are strangely silent here."

In commenting on "trying the spirits," and in view of I Timothy 4:1, A. E. Ruark, in *Falsities of Modern Tongues* (printed by Prairie Bible Institute), writes: "They seek to speak in tongues with the expectation that it is by 'the baptism of the Holy Spirit.' They thereby put themselves at the disposal of a demon spirit which may give the gift of tongues as a manifestation of this false doctrine."

Dr. Ruark states that he has personally talked with the spirits while they were using human voices, the voices of born-again children of God. He has received direct response from these spirits through the medium of the human voice. He believes that the greater part of "speaking in tongues" is done through evil spirits. He declares that statistics of two large mental institutions in the United States show that between eighty and ninety percent of the inmates are from branches of the church which practice speaking in tongues. How demons can gain submission of the mind is dealt with in his booklet. It is a revealing and frightening book and should help Christians to see why they should have nothing to do with this movement. This author continues:

Those who have spoken in tongues under demon power are subject to nervousness. They become impatient and irritable. At the same time, they boast of great spiritual power. They cannot submit to opposition or correction. They are intolerant and very dogmatic. They become extremely touchy when anything is done or said which disapproves, or corrects speaking in tongues. "The wisdom that is from above is. . . easy to be intreated" (James 3:17).

The tongues people are ensnaring many women. There is a new group called Aglow Fellowships. They are for women only and their motto is, "Women Aglow for Jesus." It is a charismatic movement. This warning is from Dr. Robert Gromacki of Cedarville College in *The Baptist Bulletin,* who continues, "Their publishing houses are becoming very aggressive" and are pushing the movement. He then reminds us that Logos International, The Bethany Fellowship of Minneapolis and Creation House, among others, are charismatic publishers. He reminds us that Corrie ten Boom is in the movement, and informs us that the Melodyland School of Theology on the West Coast is a tongues institution. So we need to be aware of what we are reading and who we listen to—many good people are being misled in these days of religious deception.

Thank God, there is a divine alternative, something very wonderful that the charismatics have missed! Let's move over into "Beulah Land" in our final Chapter.

Chapter 11

"BEULAH LAND!" — WHAT THE CHARISMATICS ARE MISSING!

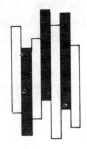

I'm living on the mountain,
Underneath a cloudless sky,
I'm drinking at the fountain
That never shall run dry;
O yes! I'm feasting on the manna
From a bountiful supply,
For I am dwelling in Beulah Land!

–C. Austin Miles

Thank God, there is a divine alternative to the charismatic movement! Jesus came to give life and to give it "more abundantly." He has a life of victory, a Beulah Land life, for every one of us. "If any man thirst, let him come unto me and drink," Christ said, assuring us that if we do, there will be "rivers of living water" flowing from our lives (John 7:37,38). "This spake he of the Spirit, which they that believe on him should receive" (John 7:39).

An ad by charismatics in a West Virginia newspaper features David J. duPlessis, one of the modern leaders in the tongues movement, as "Mr. Pentecost" and "Mr. Peacemaker," but I'm here to tell you that the Lord Jesus is the real Peacemaker and He is the one from whom we receive the gift of the Spirit when we are saved (Acts 2:38; Acts 5:32). Indeed, "If any man have not the Spirit of Christ, he is none of his" (Romans 8:9).

So the Holy Spirit *resides* in every true believer, every truly saved person (see John 14:16,17). Our bodies are the *temples* of the Holy Spirit (I Corinthians 6:19).

We are *born* of the Spirit when we are saved (John 3:6), and *baptized* by the Spirit into one body (I Corinthians 12:13).

Thus *indwelt* by the Spirit, we are led by the Spirit (Romans 8:14), *taught* of the Spirit (John 14:26), we *walk* in the Spirit (Galatians 5:16), and we are *sealed* by the Spirit unto the day of redemption (Ephesians 4:30). What a glorious possession! Not just preachers and missionaries, but students, housewives, businessmen, young people—yea all born-again ones—need to know these precious truths.

How tragic that many of us have not been living up to our potential as believers and have allowed the "charisma" confusion to get such a foothold. How sad that many today are so ignorant of the Bible as to substitute a fleshly "experience" for the truth of God's holy Word.

Many ill-taught Christians are sidetracked from the main issue of soul winning by "tongues." And many lost people, we fear, are being sidetracked into a spurious, religious "experience" instead of finding salvation by grace through faith in the finished work of Christ. Dr. McGee states, "You are saying a dangerous thing when you suggest that I must now go to the Holy Spirit, come around to the back door, and He'll slip me something that Jesus did not give me. You are saying that my Lord is accursed when you do that" (see I Corinthians 12:3). Truly, we get nothing from the Holy Spirit that we do not receive through the Lord Jesus Christ.

We need desperately today to "*try* the spirits whether they are of God." This is a command from the Lord, for everything religious, emotional and exciting is not necessarily of God at all!

When we find that a religious system is in error and that it is yoked up in fellowship with the ungodly, with modernists, Romanists, and others who are unscriptural, then the command of God is plain—we are to "come out" and "be separate!" (I Corinthians 6:14,17). We are to "have no fellowship with the unfruitful works of darkness, but rather reprove them" (Ephesians 5:11).

Writing in a "tongues" publication, one charismatic writer is supposedly telling the "good" that comes from "speaking with tongues." He proceeds to say that it is a scriptural *evidence* of the baptism of the Spirit (which it is not); he states that it gives *assur-*

ance of salvation, that men may thus speak "*supernaturally*," that we can with tongues "pray in the Spirit," that it is spiritual *worship*, that it is God's promised *rest,* that it is part of the spiritual *equipment* for the church, and that it is valuable as an evidence of faith in the Word and "the Great Commission." Exactly the opposite is true, as we learn when we see what the Bible really teaches about the Spirit-filled life!

What are the charismatics missing? Let us see:

The same Christian who is born of, indwelt by, taught of, led by and sealed with the Spirit is also commanded to be "*filled* with" the Spirit (Ephesians 5:18). This filling takes place when a Bible-taught Christian simply yields himself to the Lord, thus presenting his body in a definite act of surrender. Romans 6 and Romans 12:1,2 tell us exactly how it is done and what is involved. The teachings of Christ in the Bible and the letters to the New Testament churches give all the details.

When a born-again Christian is thus *filled* with the Spirit, he will have four wonderful new things that the charismatics are missing.

(1) NEW PERCEPTION and understanding of the Bible. His Bible will become a new book. Instead of getting into a rut with a few portions of Acts and two chapters in I Corinthians, he will find a veritable gold mine of riches throughout the whole Bible. Oh, the riches of the Word! He will rejoice in the Spirit Himself, not in "sign gifts." He will be sensitive to the

Spirit's leading, not only in his understanding of the Bible but in his own personal life. The great things of the Word will take their rightful place in his (or her) thinking.

Theodore Epp says, "The reason I refer to the charismatic movement as a form of ecumenism is that major doctrinal differences are often overlooked by those in the movement as long as a person has seemingly experienced the gifts of the Spirit—particularly the baptism of the Spirit and speaking in tongues." When a person becomes truly Spirit-filled, he can no longer overlook, bypass or ignore the blessed truths that are fundamental in the Word of God. The person thus filled will have new perception.

(2) NEW PEACE AND JOY. "Joy unspeakable and full of glory" is the expression Peter uses in the Bible to describe the blessing and bliss of those who know that they have an inheritance reserved in Heaven for them, and that they are kept by the power of God through faith, and that even though they do not yet see Christ personally, they *believe* and therefore have this "unspeakable joy" (I Peter 1:8). "In his presence there is fulness of joy" (Psalms 16:11).

Now, instead of seeking sign gifts or tongues experiences to boost their sagging spirits and give them "assurance," they have the bare, bold and blazing promises of the Word, and on these they stand! The happy Christian is the one who knows for sure that he has "eternal life; and they shall never perish" (John 10:28), that he will never be "cast out" (John 6:37) even when he fails to be perfect, that he "hath everlasting life, and shall not come into condemnation; but is passed [already] from death unto life" (John 5:24).

He has peace and joy, then, because of the Word and its meaning to him. Which is better—mumbling "Prou pray praddy; Pa palassate pa pau pu pe; Heli terratte taw; Terrei te te-te-te; Elee lete leele luto; Imba imba imba," (actual recorded "tongues speaking"), or having the wonderful Word of God for assurance?

It will not be hard for him to take God at His Word and have the assurance of his salvation now because, with the aid of the Spirit, he is made to see that salvation is "by grace through faith" and not by works, tongues or ecstatic religious exercises. Instead of always looking within to see if he is believing enough or doing enough or repenting enough to stay saved, he will go forth in joy and victory to serve the Lord with gladness because he now knows for sure that he is eternally saved by the grace of God!

Oh, the thrill of just *believing* what God says! Forty-three times in the Gospel of John alone God says saved people have everlasting (or eternal) life by believing on Jesus. He is now not looking at an experience but at God Himself. How much better to have the rich truth of the Word than to have a "wave of warmth" from the hands of a charismatic!

(3) A NEW PRAYER LIFE. Now real, intercessory prayer is hard work. Jabbering would

be much easier. But the Christian cannot set "prayer wheels turning" and go on doing his own pleasure, meanwhile. The Spirit-taught and Spirit-filled Christian realizes in a new and blessed way that God is his Heavenly Father and that he is God's child, His forever! Instead of getting "out of one's mind" into a state of ecstatic frenzy, he enjoys actually communing with God intelligently, bringing his petition to God through Christ, and receiving the answer in glorious fashion.

A converted Pentecostal preacher, who was for twenty of his thirty-one years a minister in the tongues movement, reads from a Pentecostal book their instructions about how to seek this "baptism" of the Holy Ghost. You are told to say: "Glory to Jesus, Glory to Jesus, Glory to Jesus, Glory to Jesus, Glory to Jesus, Glory to Jesus," for two or three minutes, and then change to "I love you, Jesus" for two or three minutes, and then to "Hallelujah" for two or three minutes, and then to "Praise Father, Son and Holy Ghost" for two or three minutes, and then to a mixture of "I love you, Jesus" and "Thank you, Jesus" and "Bless the Lord," "Jesus my Saviour," and "Amen" for several minutes. If starting to stammer, the would-be "tongues speaker" is not supposed to "quench the Spirit" by trying to stop stammering, but rather encourage the stammering so it can change into "unknown tongues"! The now-converted Pentecostal pastor says that this is characteristic, this trying to be lost to the thing that is natural, "losing your mind to the circumstance," and by rapidly saying the words, you are to receive this so-called great blessing. But the man of God says that *now* he knows that we do not need to coax and beg and go through some hypnotic type of service, but if we just yield to Christ, surrender ourselves and obey the Scriptures, that the Holy Spirit will take maximum control of our lives in power and fill us (From *What About Speaking in Tongues,* an interview with Rev. Clarence Lefever by Evangelist J. Bennett Collins). Clarence Lefever says that now he has found great joy and peace in the precious presence of the Holy Spirit when he just ministers the Word without any of the interpretations of man.

Intelligent praying in one's own mother tongue to a gracious Heavenly Father who has given us hundreds of prayer promises to cash in on is an ecstasy hard to beat!

(4) A NEW POWER. Acts 1:8 tells us that the reason God gives the power of the Spirit is to make us witnesses. Jesus said if we would follow Him we would be made into "fishers of men." Christians who win souls, who witness intelligently and give the plan of salvation to hungry hearts, will find that the Holy Spirit is right there helping as He uses us to bless others. Is it any wonder that the soul winner's crown is called the "crown of rejoicing?" (I Thessalonians 2:19).

"They that be wise shall shine as the brightness of the firmament; and they that turn many to righteousness [not "talk in tongues"] as the stars for ever and ever" (Daniel 12:3).

"He that winneth souls is wise" (Proverbs 11:30).

"As my Father hath sent me, even so send I you" (John 20:21), Jesus said.

In a Roman Catholic charismatic gathering, it is said that "lively chatter and heavy cigarette smoke dispelled any thought of formality." The Spirit-filled Christian would, of course, at once know that smoking would hurt his testimony (as well as his health), and a truly saved Catholic would be constrained to come out of a false religion and seek a church where the glorious salvation of God is preached and believed.

Don W. Hillis writes:

> What, after all, is the picture one gains from a study of the early church? Is it that of a little band of people who distinguish themselves from the rest of the world by their experiences in speaking in "unknown tongues"? Or is it that of a fearless group of people who are very much in the world, though not of it—who turn the world upside down by their bold declaration of the gospel message in languages understood by their hearers? We do well to objectively and honestly face this question. (From *What Can Tongues Do for You?* by Don W. Hillis.)

Thousands of souls are being won today by Spirit-filled, intelligent Christians who realize their responsibility and the sheer privilege of winning others to Christ. This is one reason why many of our Bible-believing churches are growing and flourishing as never before.

If you do not have this blessed perception, peace and power today, why not ask God to fill you afresh with His Spirit now? Then you can sing:

> *I've reached the land of corn and wine,*
> *And all its riches freely mine;*
> *Here shines undimmed one blissful day,*
> *For all my night has passed away.*
>
> *My Saviour comes and walks with me,*
> *And sweet communion here have we;*
> *He gently leads me by His hand,*
> *For this is Heaven's borderland.*
>
> *O Beulah Land, sweet Beulah Land,*
> *As on thy highest mount I stand,*
> *I look away across the sea,*
> *Where mansions are prepared for me,*
> *And view the shining glory shore,*
> *My Heav'n, my home forevermore!*

> *–Edgar Page*

Though I have spoken honestly and plainly, it is with a sincere desire to help lead people into a knowledge of the truth. Many sweet Christians are nevertheless ill-taught and deceived. The time is short to serve the Lord and reach this sin-sick world with the glorious gospel. As Dr. Monroe Parker has said, "Pentecost was Ground-breaking Day. Now it's time to get to work!" God bless you!

Additional Help

Some sincere Christians may feel they need additional help with "tongues" or the charismatic matter. I have referred to many books in these chapters. Some, I think, are more helpful than others. For the sake of brevity, I am listing these which I feel to be among the most valuable and would give good help along certain lines. All but *The Power of Pentecost* are inexpensive paperbacks.

WHAT IS WRONG IN THE CHURCH (Vol. 2, Counterfeit Speaking in Tongues), by Alex R. Hay. Order from New Testament Missionary Union, 256 Oak Street, Audubon, N.J. 08106; or from the Elms, 672 Quaker Road, Welland, Ontario, Canada.

THE STRIFE OF TONGUES, by Kurt Koch. Order from Kregal Publishers, Grand Rapids, Mich. 49503; or Spanish World Gospel Broadcasting, Inc., Box 335, Winona Lake, Ind. 46590.

SPEAKING WITH TONGUES (Series of booklets) by Spiros Zodhiates. Order from American Mission to Greeks, Inc., Ridgefield, N.J. 07657.

SPEAKING WITH TONGUES (paper), by John R. Rice, and THE POWER OF PENTECOST (cloth), by John R. Rice. Order from

Sword of the Lord, Box 1099, Murfreesboro, Tenn. 37130.

SPEAKING IN TONGUES, by Lehman Strauss, Bible Study Time, Box 6191, Philadelphia, Penn. 19115.

BIBLICAL CONCLUSIONS CONCERNING TONGUES, by C. Norman Sellers, 2300 N. W. 135th Street, Miami, Fla. 33167.

THE NINE GIFTS OF THE SPIRIT ARE NOT IN THE CHURCH TODAY, by B. F. Cate, Regular Baptist Press, 1800 Oakton Blvd., Des Plaines, Ill. 60018.

FALSITIES OF MODERN TONGUES, by A. E. Ruark. Order from Prairie Bible Institute, Three Hills, Alberta, Canada.

TONGUES, GLOSSOLALIA AND CHARIS-MATIC RENEWAL IN THE LIGHT OF THE BIBLE Tract, by E. L. Bynum, Box 3327, Lubbock, Tex. 79411.

CHARISMATIC CONFUSION, by Paul Van Gorder, The Radio Bible Class, P.O. Box 22, Grand Rapids, Mich. 49501.